The Missing Button

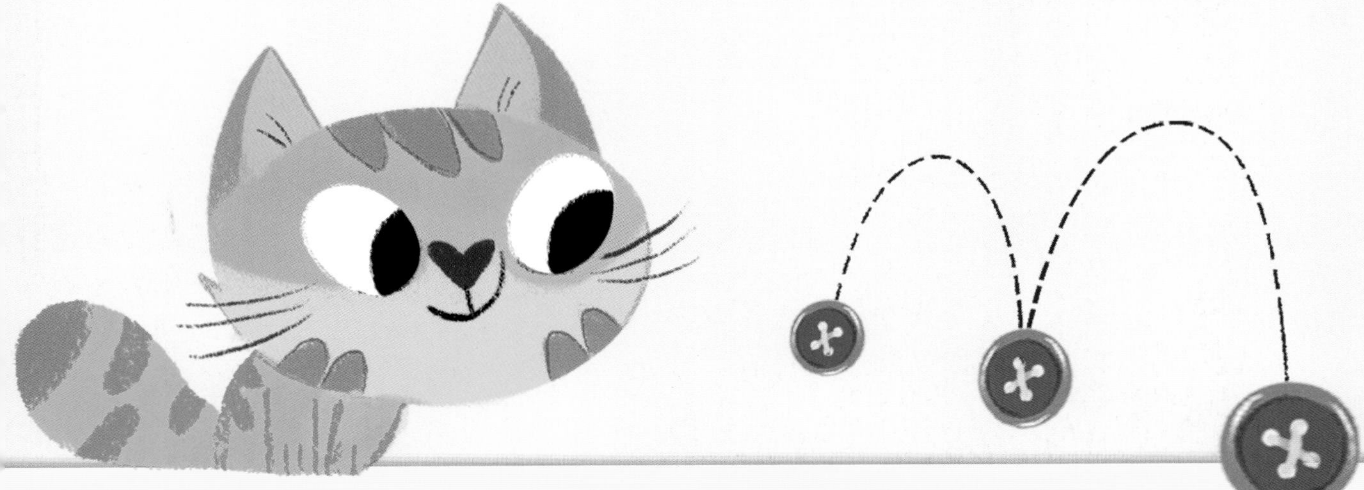

Written by Sarah Loader
Illustrated by Valeria Issa

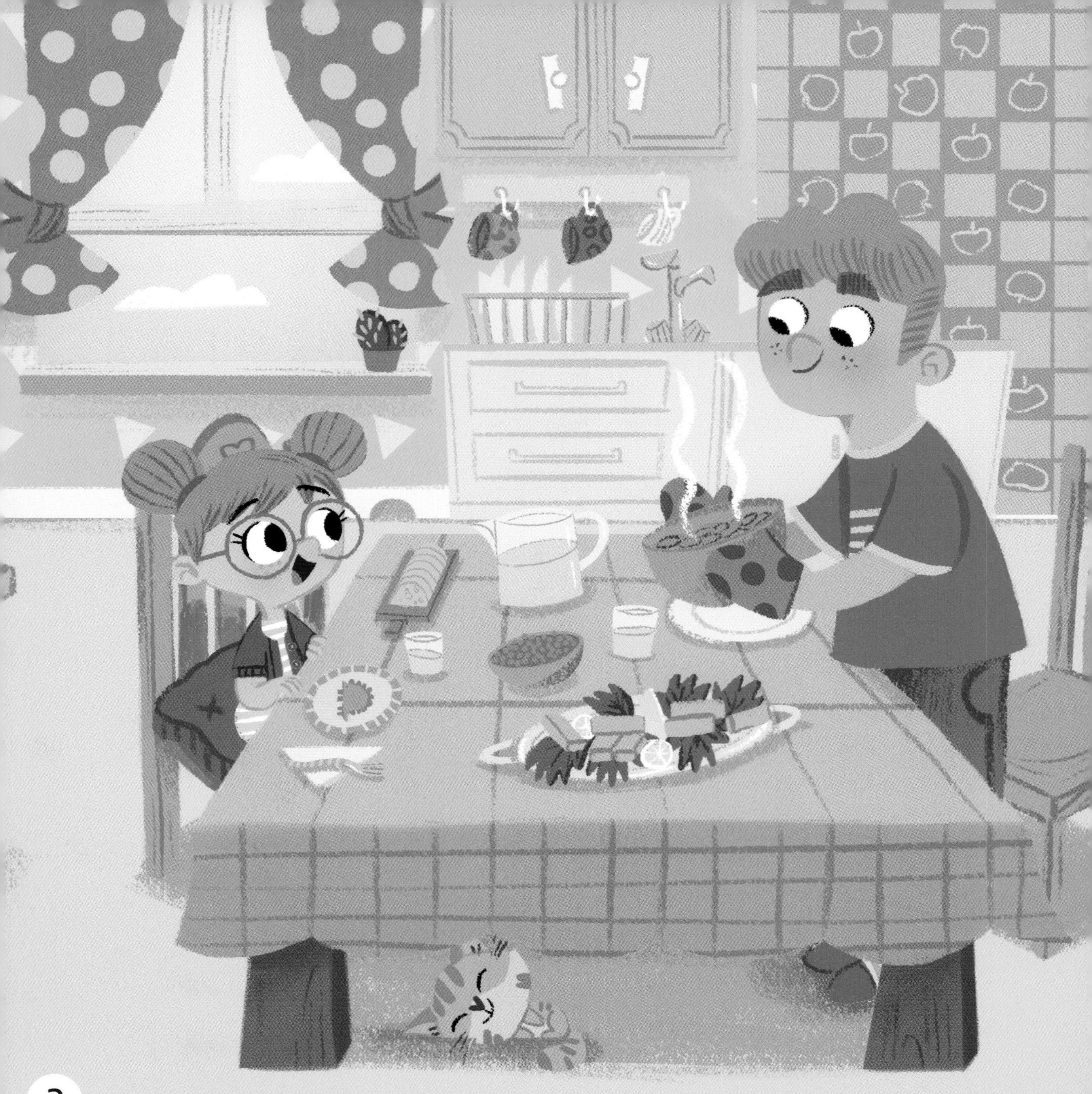

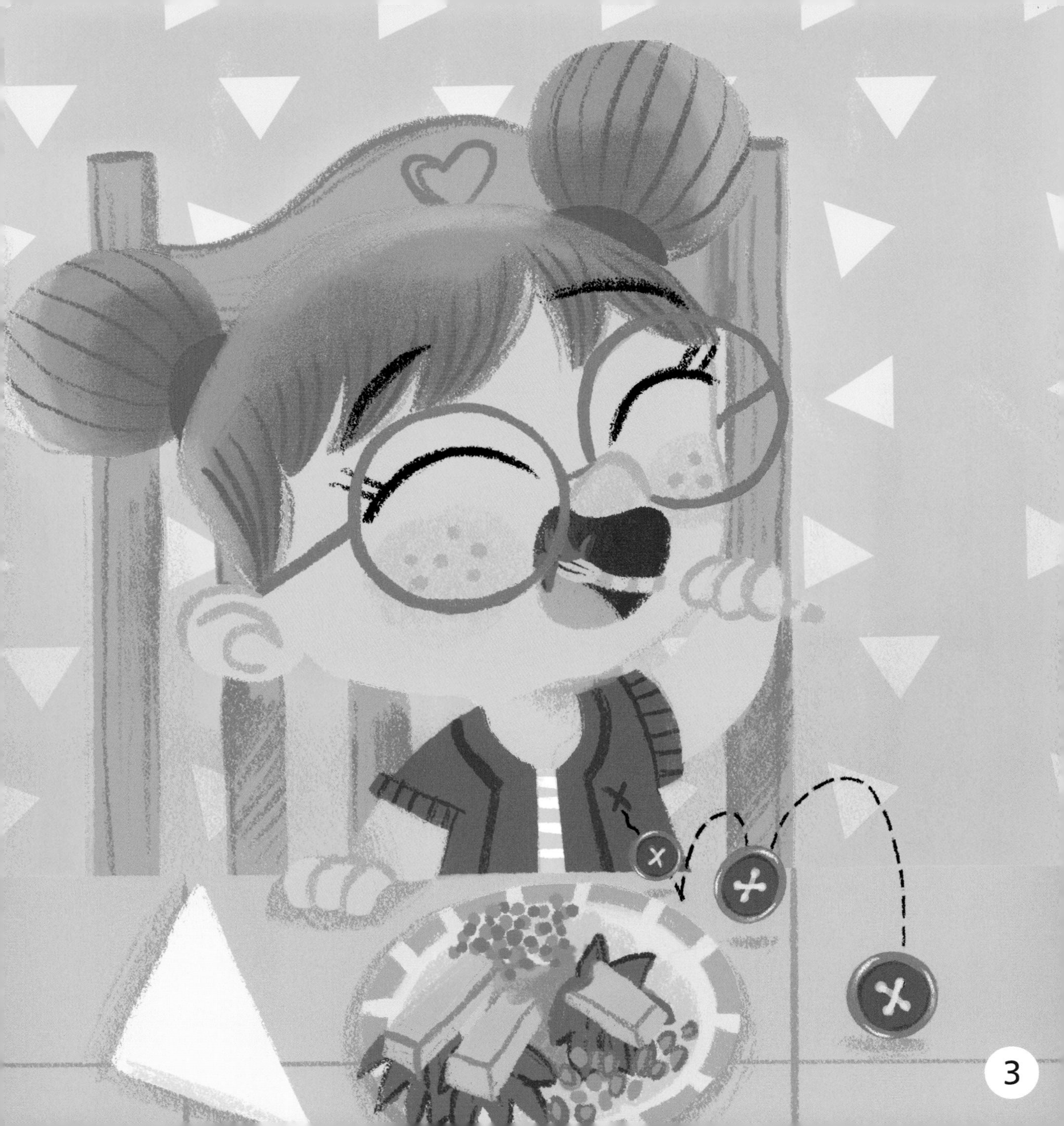

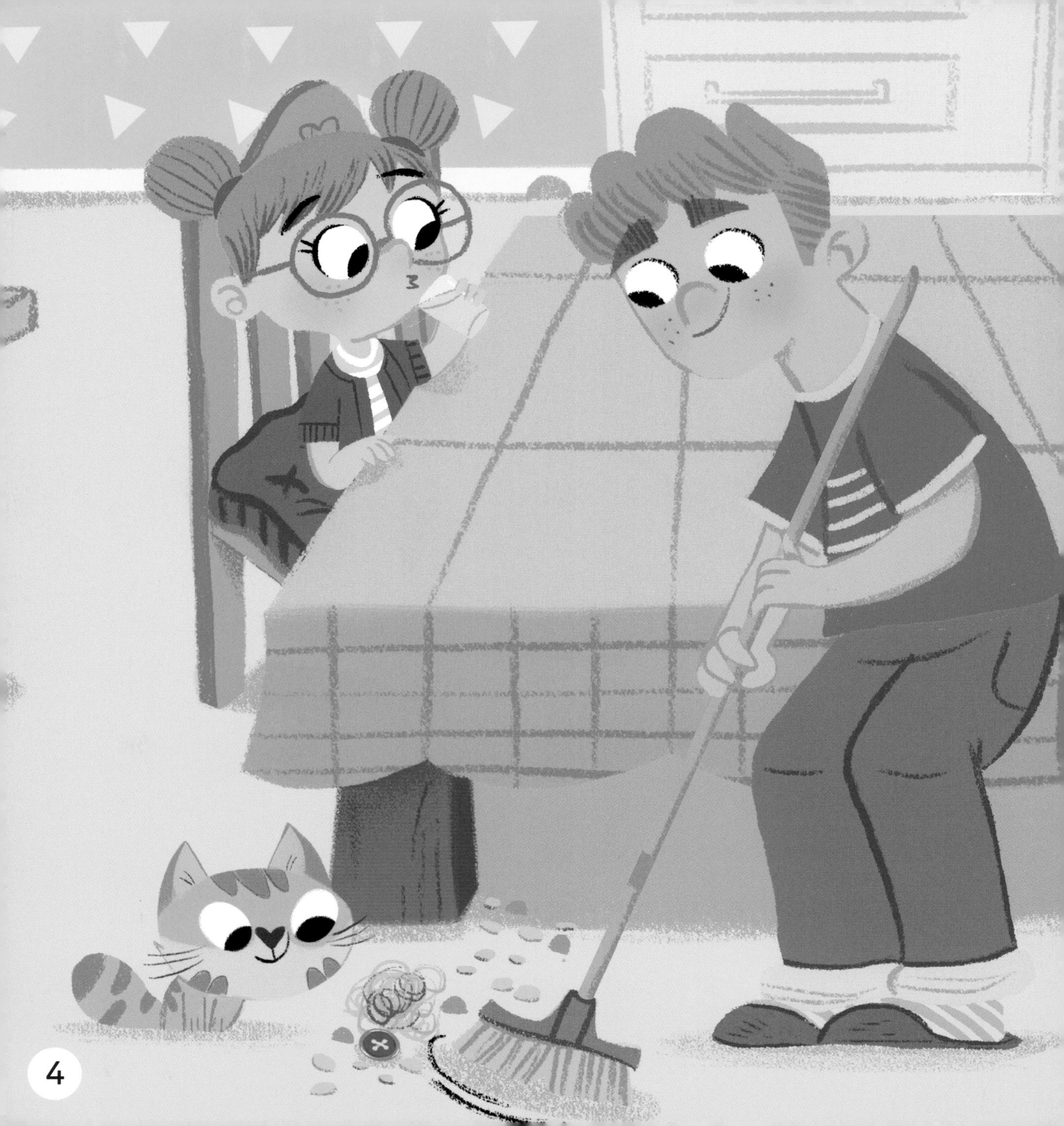

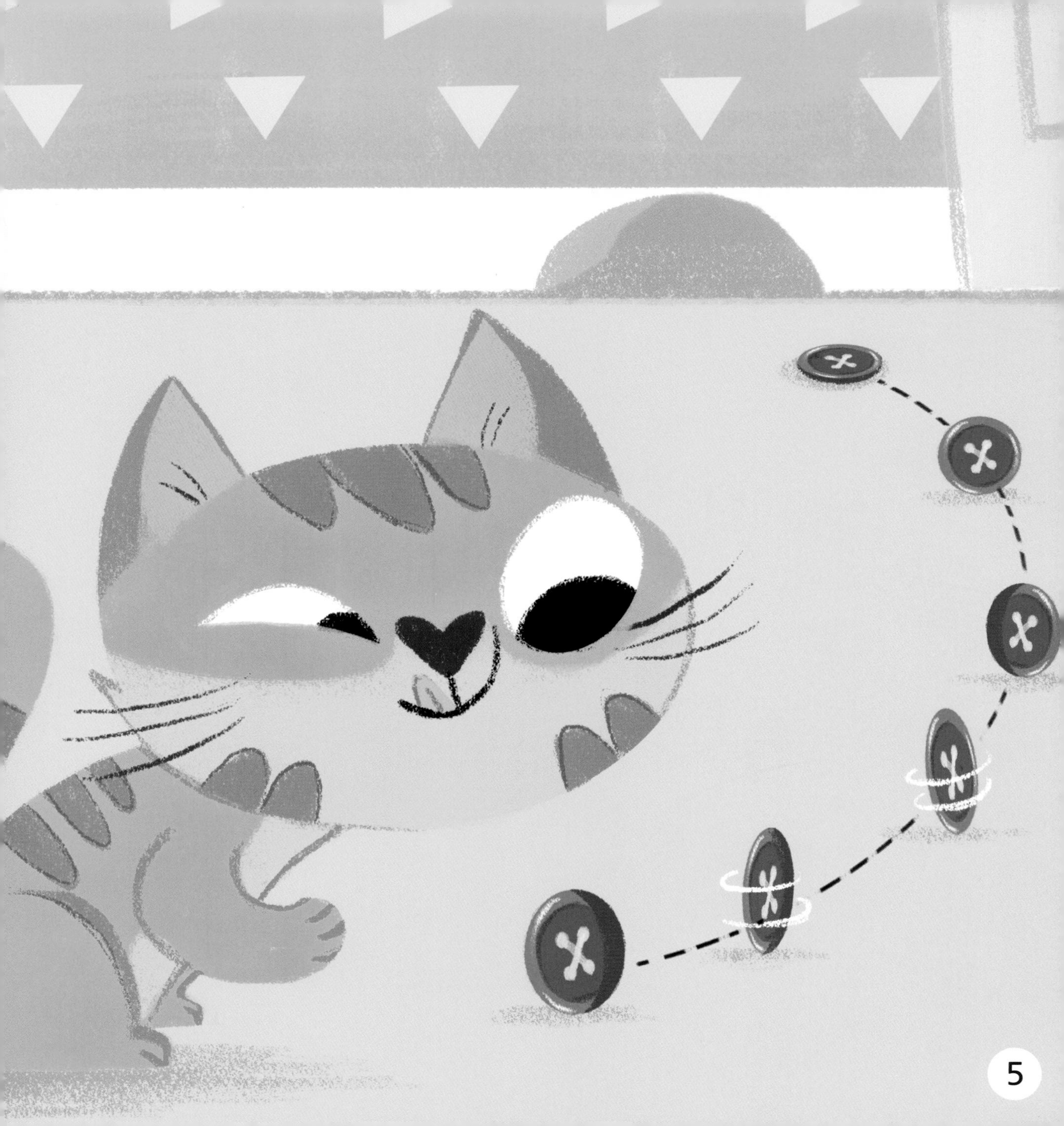

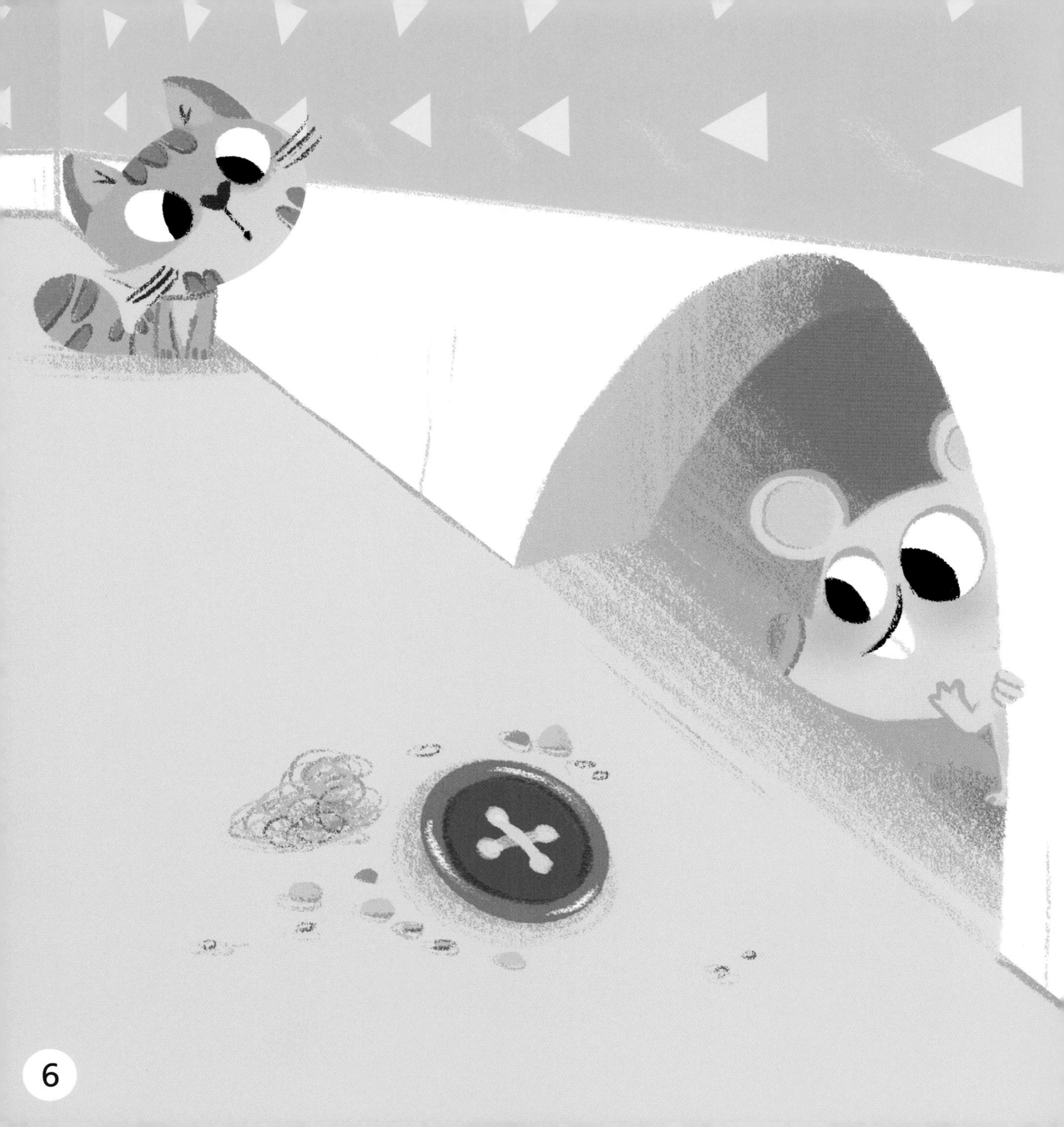

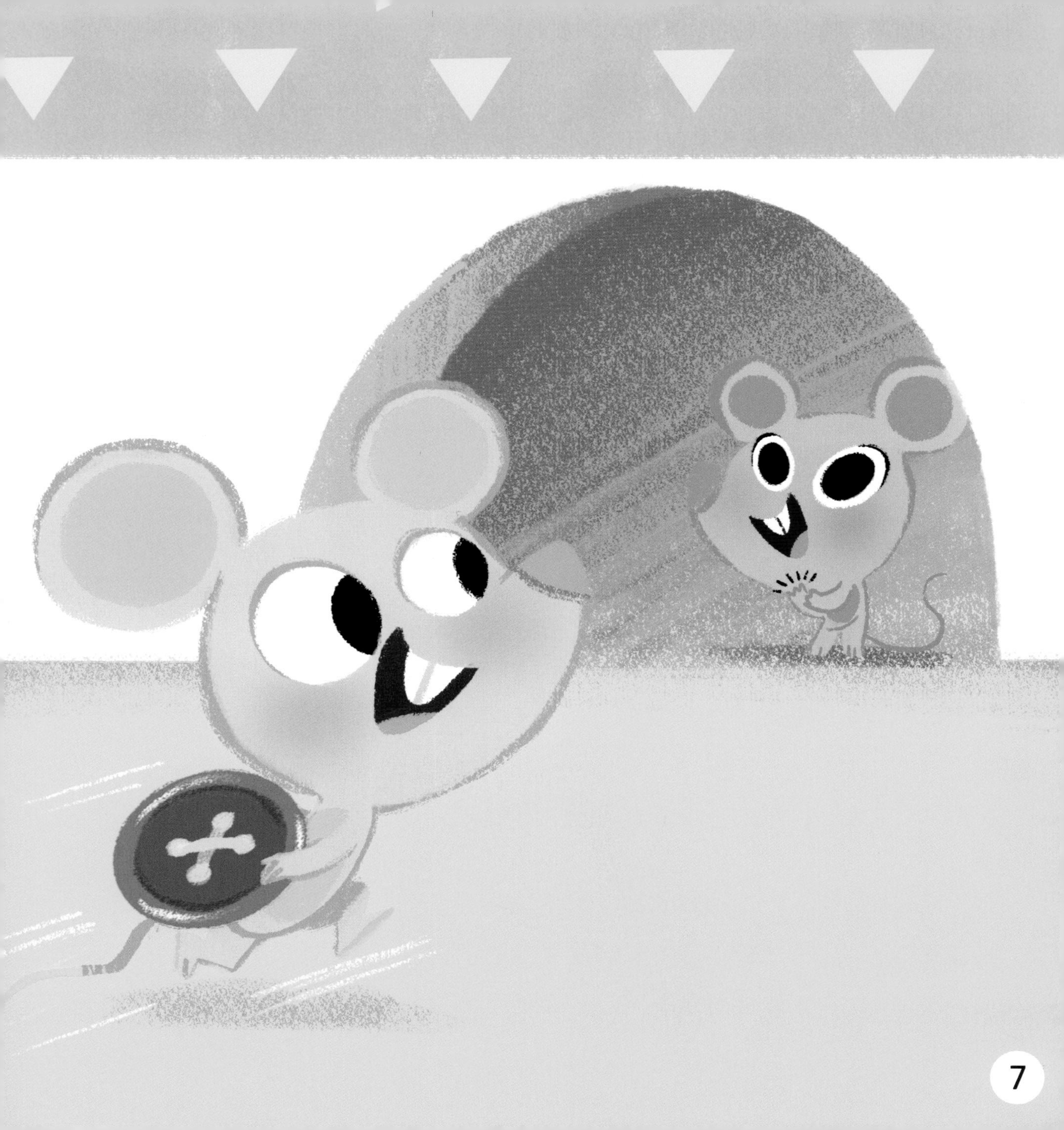

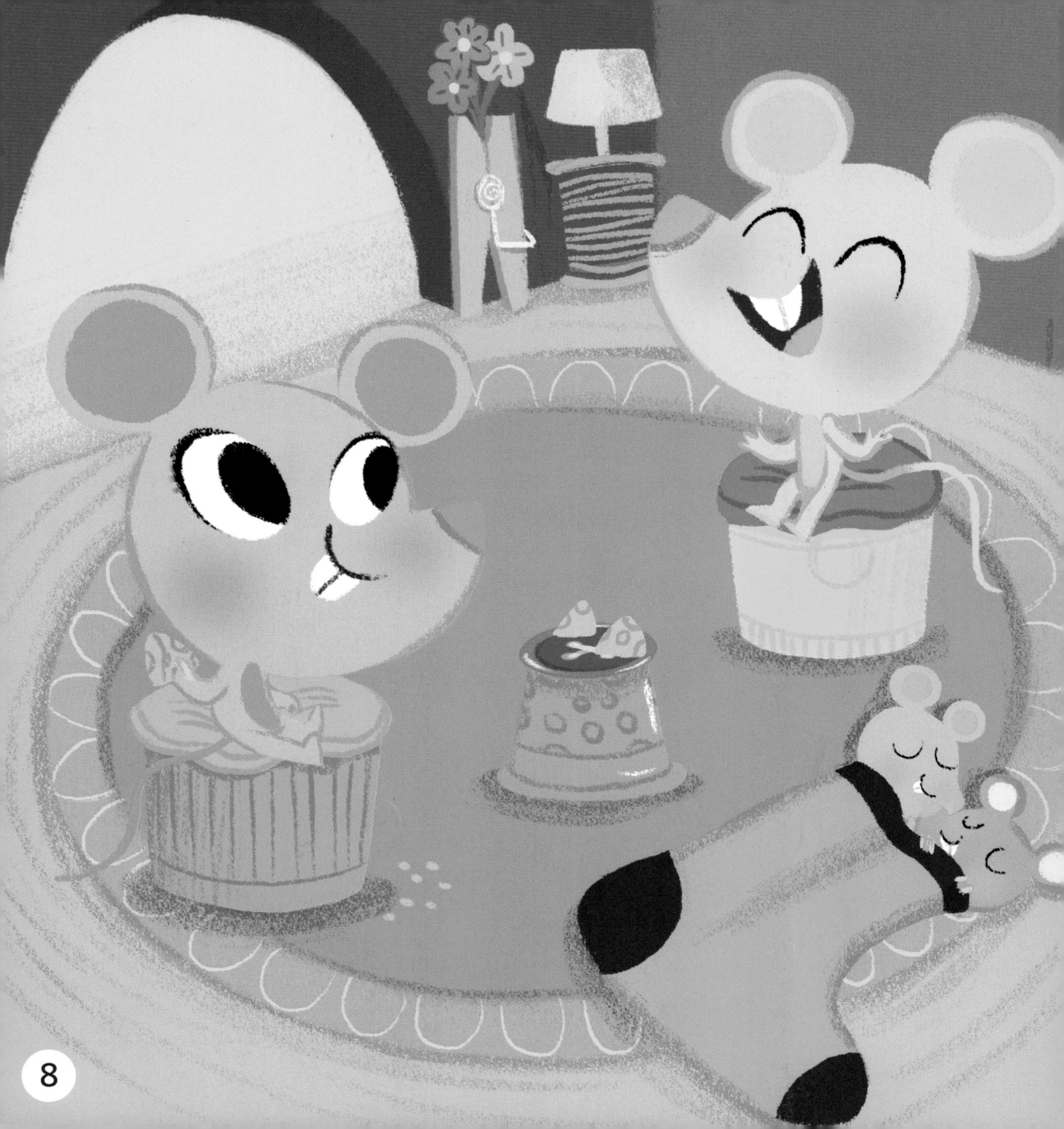